Your Cartoon Time

This book belongs to:

(Self-portrait)

Paula Low

(Signature)

About the author

Rolf Harris was born in Perth, Western Australia. He's lived in England for over thirty years now and is known and loved throughout the world as a musician, singer, writer, entertainer and, of course, artist.

Your Cartoon Time

Rolf Harris

KNIGHT BOOKS
Hodder and Stoughton

Copyright © Rolf Harris 1986

First published by Knight Books 1986

British Library C.I.P.

Harris, Rolf
Your cartoon time.
1. Australian wit and humor, Pictorial
I. Title
741.5'994   NC1759

ISBN 0-340-39223-1

This book is sold subject to the condition that
it shall not, by way of trade or otherwise, be
lent, re-sold, hired out or otherwise circulated
without the publisher's prior consent in any
form of binding or cover other than that in
which it is published and without a similar
condition including this condition being
imposed on the subsequent purchaser.

Printed and bound in Great Britain for
Hodder and Stoughton Paperbacks, a
division of Hodder and Stoughton Ltd.,
Mill Road, Dunton Green, Sevenoaks,
Kent (Editorial Office: 47 Bedford
Square, London, WC1 3DP) by
Richard Clay (The Chaucer Press) Ltd.,
Bungay, Suffolk. Photoset by
Rowland Phototypesetting Ltd.,
Bury St Edmunds, Suffolk.

Contents

Here is a marvellous bold lino cut based on my "Rolfaroo" character.

This example was created by Shaun Easton aged 10.

Introduction

So you want to draw cartoons?

Do you just want to be able to copy the cartoon characters you see on the screen and in comic strips, or do you want to be able to create your own cartoon characters?

Whatever the answer, there are ways I can help and other ways where you can, and must, help yourself if you are going to be any good.

What are my qualifications, you ask. Well, I've been drawing since I can remember. I use cartoon drawings in every facet of my life, and I get *tremendous* pleasure and fun out of illustrating everything – letters, documents, envelopes, postcards – you name it, if there's a space, I'll draw on it.

I see so many children who are really gifted at drawing action and expression and different characters, but by the time they get into their teens they've shut all that side of themselves away and have lost that wonderful source of pleasure for themselves, their friends and their families.

I think it very sad, and such a waste of that special talent that's been handed to you. Drawing, painting and self-expression are as important in life as maths, geography, history and computer technology, so let's all develop our talents.

You may say, 'I can't draw!'

All you have to do is look closely at all the publications using hundreds of cartoons a week. Some of the artists are superb at figure work and draughtsmanship, but as many of them are not so good. They've just taken what they have, like a terrific sense of humour and tons of enthusiasm, and have put down that idea in their own special and very recognisable style, and it has tickled our funnybone. Just have a look at some of the cartoons and pieces of artwork at the end of the book and look at all the different

7

styles – there is definitely a place for you in there somewhere.

Back to you and your cartoons; the first thing is to draw, draw, draw at every available opportunity.

There is no special mystery that I can solve about the right materials to use. Use whatever is to hand – pens, pencils, crayons, felt-tipped markers – anything that will make a mark on paper. Some felt-tipped pens with a spirit base will soak into most paper as if it were blotting paper, so with those you've got to work really quickly and avoid leaving the felt tip resting on the paper or you'll finish up with a big circular 'blot' there.

Use any paper you can get, but it is best if it has no lines printed on it. You may approach printers to see if they have any offcuts of paper they were going to throw away that you could have, or quite often picture framers have quantities of small square or oblong offcuts from picture frame mounts that would normally just go into the dustbin.

Ask . . . they can only say no, and they might be thrilled to help you.

Right, let's draw some cartoons.

Of course, I don't know how old you are, what sort of drawing you can already do, or how good you are at what you draw . . . so, let me start at the earliest possible stage and you can pick it up wherever you want to.

Have fun, that's the important thing!

1
Stick figure action

To me, the most important thing to get into a cartoon is the action. Everyone wants to know what the person in the cartoon is *doing*.

It's no good having a perfect drawing of a person if that person is just stuck there like a wooden dummy. It is better to have a 'not so perfect' drawing where you can see what the person is *doing*. Look at these two drawings and pick which you like the best.

I think you will agree that the running figure is more fun – even though his hands are not perfect and you're not sure what sort of clothes he's wearing, you can enjoy that running action . . . you know what he's doing, and he looks excited to be doing it. When you look at it you feel that excitement.

Most people when they start drawing seem to draw people from the front so that they can see the whole face and both arms and both legs.

They are all very good drawings, but the next step from here is to get some *action* happening.

Try drawing the most simple figure you can – just a head, a stick for the body – two sticks for arms and two for legs. If you like you can put a bunch of little sticks for fingers and a flat, short stick for each foot. There you have it . . . very simple, and yet you can see that the person is standing astride with arms stretched and the fingers spread out. Unless you put features on the head you can't tell if the figure is facing you or facing the other way . . .

So . . . draw eyes, nose and mouth simply.

See how many different positions you can draw of a stick person facing you. I'll start with a few to show what I mean. Have a look at the different expressions on the faces.

Have a look at the last figure. The legs are crossed but you really don't know which is in front and which is behind. If I draw it again can you tell now? Yes! You can *see* that the bent leg is in front of the straight one because I've stopped drawing the straight one just for a tiny distance where it goes behind the front leg.

See if you can draw some figures where arms and legs cross so that everyone knows which is in front and which is behind. Here are some from me.

You can see that I've added a few things like sticks, spears, ropes, rackets, balls and bows and arrows to the figures to add interest to the action.

Have you noticed that some of the figures are half turning to one side or the other? It is quite difficult to show some actions if you look only from the front.

Let me draw a few from both the front and the side to show you what I mean.

FRONT

SIDE

FRONT

SIDE

FRONT

SIDE

So . . . do as many side-on drawings of actions as you can think of. When you are drawing try to make the action as exciting as possible.

A runner moving like this

is not as exciting as one running like this.

13

If you really want the runner to look as if he's trying –

make his mouth open as if he's gasping for breath – and his eyebrows raised. You could shade the cheeks to make him look hot and do some drops of perspiration coming from his face and body. I think I'll draw his ear in because I miss it a bit.

It would be even better if you had something chasing after him to give him a reason to move.

See how many different actions you can think of to draw from a side-on view. I'll draw a few, but you will think of *lots* more.

15

2
Bring the sticks alive

The big trouble with stick figures, as we've already seen, is that when you get a lot of arms mixed up you really don't know which arm is in front and which is behind. The drawing gets confused.

Try thickening up the stick arms and legs like this.

Now you can see which leg is in front and which is behind and the same with the arms.

Try the two sparring – that's much better isn't it!

Look at some more stick figures doing different things like playing billiards, football, tennis . . .

. . . or doing some swimming.

Clothe all those stick figures with legs and arms and costumes.

Now you can see the body action in a much clearer way.

If you need some help in thickening up the stick figures you can always draw the sticks in very lightly and then draw the solid arms and legs and body around the faint stick figures.

3

Begin the action

Look back at the billiard player, the footballer and the
tennis player – they do look a bit weak and feeble, as if
they are really not trying. You should always try to
exaggerate the action; make it larger than life.

I suppose the billiard player
is reasonably well drawn
because those players don't
get very animated when playing, but the footballer could
be really belting that ball
away and the tennis player
could be really trying. Somehow his racket-holding arm
is wrong. Try holding your
arm up as if you are holding a racket just prior to whack-

ing that ball. See if you can
visualise what it looks like –
now, draw it! You'll see I
made a couple of attempts at
the tennis player serving.
The first one still looked too
pussy-footed. What I did was,
I stood up and went through
the action of serving and
realised that my right elbow
was right up at the top of my head, my chest was thrown

out as I flung the ball high
with my left hand and one
knee was slightly bent so
that just the toe of my foot
was on the ground.

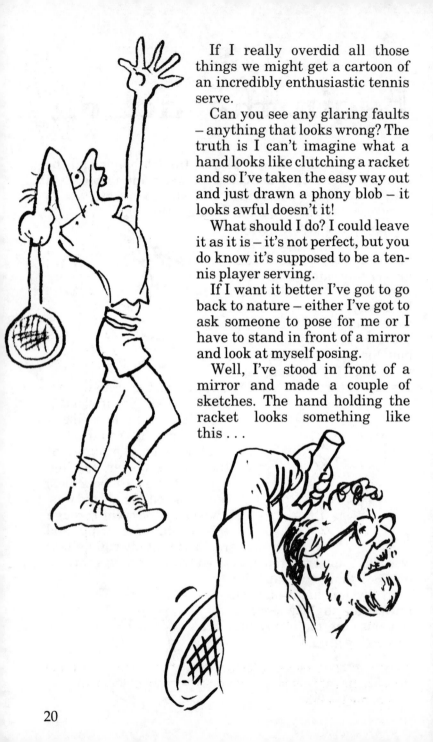

If I really overdid all those things we might get a cartoon of an incredibly enthusiastic tennis serve.

Can you see any glaring faults – anything that looks wrong? The truth is I can't imagine what a hand looks like clutching a racket and so I've taken the easy way out and just drawn a phony blob – it looks awful doesn't it!

What should I do? I could leave it as it is – it's not perfect, but you do know it's supposed to be a tennis player serving.

If I want it better I've got to go back to nature – either I've got to ask someone to pose for me or I have to stand in front of a mirror and look at myself posing.

Well, I've stood in front of a mirror and made a couple of sketches. The hand holding the racket looks something like this . . .

and the arm throwing the ball up in the air looks something like this.

I realise I've picked the wrong leg to bend – the one that does the slight lifting off the ground is the one on the opposite side of the body from the serving hand.

It looks a bit like this.

So now I have some information with which to do a much more believable cartoon of a man serving at tennis.

Let me try one.

This drawing is nowhere near as much fun as the earlier one was – maybe I'm trying to be too accurate and too clever. The drawing is starting to look like a very bad anatomy lesson. I must get more fun into it!

Exaggerate more!!

That's better.

Do you notice I've made the figure much shorter and more cartoon-like rather than stick to the actual proportions of a normal person? (I'll talk about proportions in chapters 7 and 9.)

You notice also that I've gone back to the blob for the hand holding the racket. I feel the action is more important than the accuracy of the drawing. You may notice I've got him leaning forward a bit too. You sort of get the feeling he may fall forward if he doesn't quickly take a step – good!

4
Underline the action

If you want to make those action drawings really come to life there are all sorts of little things you can add to give the illusion of even more movement taking place.

First you can put some little lines, like small visual echoes, to show where the object was a few seconds ago. It's a bit like blinking rapidly and seeing four pictures of where the ball was before it got to its present position. Here's an example.

You could have some little lines by the top of the hand to show that it had also moved. I've added a few behind his head, his other hand and his foot to show that they are moving too.

If you wanted to show the player to be moving rapidly across the floor rather than just ambling – you would first need to have him leaning at more of an angle, and he would need to be in a running position as well – like this . . .

23

Let me draw that again with all the little visual 'echoes' drawn in.

Now – if we wanted to show some real speed we could draw some horizontal lines streaming out behind him almost like the slipstream of an aeroplane. On top of that we could show some little puffs of dust left behind and we could have him all red-faced – gasping for air and with drops of perspiration flying from his face.

Let's try that.

Did you like the startled bird? Nice touch, I thought – really gave the impression the runner had gone past so fast, and created such turbulence in the air, that the bird's flying had become a panic-stricken flutter in an endeavour to stay airborne.

One other way to give a terrific impression of speed is to have whatever is moving totally off the ground. This effect is achieved quite simply by drawing a shadow just beneath the moving person or object or animal.

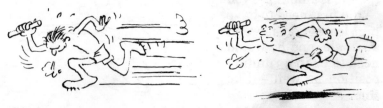

See how much faster the second runner appears to be going because we suddenly realise that he is off the ground altogether – totally unstable – and must be going really fast or he'd fall over.

What would happen if I actually drew one of the runner's feet touching the ground?

Somehow he looks as if he's suddenly standing still . . . and a strong wind is blowing past him . . .

. . . or even as if he's suddenly stood on a piece of board which is skating away on the ice carrying him with it. Maybe he's solid on his left foot and pushing with his right.

Let's have another look at the footballer I drew earlier. I could certainly make him more enthusiastic.

Better. Now . . .

. . . put a little shadow under him . . . magic! Suddenly he's got *both* feet off the ground!

We could make him red-faced and panting to heighten the feeling of hard work and exertion . . . and some lines to show that he's run up to that position. See how much harder he's kicked the ball that last time. Why? Simply because I've drawn straight lines between his foot and the ball – in the previous drawings I did curved lines, showing that the ball was just casually booted and had gone in a looping curve away from the foot.

Have a look again at the runner and the dog – not stick figures anymore, but real solid figures. I've put some lines around him to re-inforce the action.

If you're not sure how people or animals look when they're moving, you can always get some photos of them in action – or even watch them and try to sketch the shape quickly.

Try to draw all the action figures you can, adding little lines to show movement, and others to show speed.

The tennis player serving for example. Without the lines of action he could be just scratching his head with the handle of the racket.

Draw as many movements as you can with humans and animals.

5

Get the sequence right

I was just going to start re-drawing all the action stick figures that we did before, but this time with thick arms, legs and bodies, and suddenly I realised something that I do as a matter of course, which may not have occurred to you.

When you are doing a drawing which shows arms and legs crossing one in front of the other, you should draw whatever is closest to you first. Look at this figure.

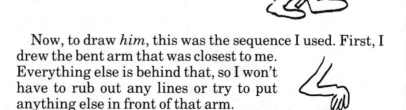

Now, to draw *him*, this was the sequence I used. First, I drew the bent arm that was closest to me. Everything else is behind that, so I won't have to rub out any lines or try to put anything else in front of that arm.

Next . . . what do we have? Right . . . the body and the leg closest to me, that is, the bent leg. You see that I've made the body go behind the bent arm.

Can you see what would have happened if I had drawn the body and the bent leg first and then tried to draw that bent arm on top? It would look like this . . .

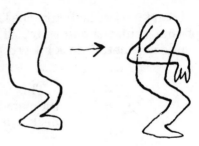

. . . and then I would have had to rub out those lines where the body is supposed to be behind the bent arm.

The next thing I would draw would be the straight leg.

Then, the furthest thing away from me would be the arm holding the walking stick. See how the stick goes *behind* the leg.

Now add the head and he's finished.

THANK GOODNESS FOR THAT! I THOUGHT I'D NEVER SEE WHERE I WAS GOING!

I don't particularly like the fact that the head sits on top of that round shoulder bit. If I was drawing it again I would do a better neck bit I think – I'll show you.

This time I've put the head on at the same time as the body, so the neck looks more natural.

Now I'll add that final arm and the stick. The poor fellow got older and better dressed as the cartoon progressed.

Notice the little lines around his foot as he feels for the step – it all helps. Also the slightly shaky lines of his legs and arms seem to indicate that he is old and a bit shaky himself.

This is what it would look like if I had drawn the things furthest away from me first. You can see I would need to rub out and clean up a lot of lines before that drawing would work at all.

So, always start by drawing what is closest to you. It helps if you can close your eyes and imagine the picture before you start, then, in your mind's eye, you can see all the problems and avoid them.

Right . . . to work . . . well, it's not work, is it? It's *fun*!

Let's get on with turning all our stick figures into real cartoons.

Remember the first one on p. 10?

 Now, you don't have to be brilliant. I've just got a rough idea of his hands. I've imagined him in a sloppy old pair of shoes and shorts. I think we should put some ears on the face  and maybe shirts or dresses and long hair for the girls we decide to draw. These were the stick figures from p. 11.

I'll thicken them up.

31

What do you think of the last one? Something looks wrong – maybe the bent leg is too long or the foot he has all his weight on is facing the wrong way. Let me try that drawing again – maybe the bent leg will have to face down to the ground at the knee, then the bottom part of the leg can come across properly and not look too long – I'll try.

No! Even unfinished it's looking odd. I drew the arm that was going to hold the leg before I decided where the leg should go – I'll do the bent leg first and *then* ... the

arm. Another thing ... when you're standing on one leg, your head must be directly above the foot you're standing on, otherwise you start to fall over. That's better – you can see he's distressed and has been hopping about holding his ankle.

Shall we do some more?

Good. Here's the next group from p. 12.

If you make a mistake don't rub it out and go over and over it trying to make each cartoon a perfect drawing. It will just finish up a mess. A mistake is all right – everybody makes mistakes – leave it there so you can see where you went wrong and do another drawing. This time, try to learn from that mistake and do it the way you wanted it to be in the first place.

A TRICKY ONE

See how the rope is in front of the legs in one drawing. (I drew from the top, down to the hands and shorts, *then* drew the rope, and then the legs going behind that rope.) And the rope is behind the legs in this last drawing (I drew the rope last, after the legs were drawn). A drawing of him skipping with both feet off the ground would be good. How would you draw that? Visualise the action, even get up and do a pretend skip just imagining where the rope would be. Got it in your mind? Right! First do a stick figure, see if it works, see where the problems are, and then do your real cartoon.

If you are skipping a rope it seems to me that your elbows are tucked into your hips and your forearms are horizontal and only your wrists are moving the rope around in a big circle, big enough to go right over your head and under your bent legs. *Quick* ... draw it!!!

The rope almost flattens where it hits the ground.

Let's draw those two as cartoon characters. There would be no fingers sticking out because the hands would be clutching the rope. I'll fix that – and I think I'll make it a girl skipping so I can use the position of her hair and her dress to show some action too.

I've just stood up and actually tried out the skipping action and I've got it wrong! The knees are bent when the rope is *above* you, because you've just landed on the ground. The legs are straight just after you've jumped off the ground, and your forearms are facing further down to get the rope under you.

I'll try to draw that again.

That certainly looks more like the action.

Now, turn it into thickened cartoons.

I'm not sure I like the shading on the shirt, but I'm committed now. You would probably need a lot more drawings to show the whole sequence of someone skipping – but that looks a bit better – doesn't it?

Let's finish off the other couple of stick figures we did earlier.

I got the spear a bit bent. I'll fix that!

Better!

There are still a lot of stick figures back there that we haven't turned into cartoons. Remember these from page 13?

Now that bicycle is a very difficult one. For a start, my stick figure on the bicycle looks strange. If you are going to try to draw this I think you could be excused for roughing in all the parts of the bicycle and the body in pencil first and then going over the parts you wanted to draw in ink. Remember . . . draw the things closest to you first, the things furthest away from you last.

Rough pencil.

Pen over rough pencii.

Pencil rubbed out.

Just add a few speed lines and you have it, a down-hill race!

It might make all the complicated shapes easier to understand if you filled in the bike in black like this.

I've made him go slowly up-hill – see all the bumpy echo lines to show the rough road. Notice the change of expression on his face. See how many different expressions you can draw on the faces of your cartoon figures.

Here are the next lot. First, the runner. When you look at the stick figure you can't tell which arm or which leg is in front and which is behind. Shall we make a decision? O.K. . . . the right arm is forward and the left arm is back. Draw it!
Now!!!!

We've got to a very important part and something you may not have thought of. Just walk up and down and swing your arms as you walk. As your right arm swings forward and your left arm swings back – which foot is forward? Unless you are a very awkward walker, the left leg will be moving forward as your left arm swings back. In this way the body balances itself. It's the same in running – as the *right* arm reaches forward so does the *left* leg. I'll carry on with the drawing. I've changed his facial expression and he doesn't look as serious as the first

half-finished runner looked, does he? He looks as if he's 'playing' at running – watching to see if everyone is looking at him.

I'll draw someone who is really intent on winning. He is certainly serious – look at his straight right leg driving him out of the starting blocks. What else can you see that shows how hard he's trying? His fingers are all stretching out, he's frowning in concentration as he looks ahead to the winning post, and his mouth is in a sort of snarl as he snatches a breath.

I'll draw a runner this time with the arms and legs in the reverse position, that is left arm and right leg reaching forward.

Just to see how strange it looks if I do the runner with the left arm and the left leg back and the right arm and the right leg forward. Have a look. Ah . . . well, it doesn't look too bad actually, does it? But you try to run like that – it's like someone walking all wrong – like Frankenstein's monster . . . You know moving his whole left side forward at once, then his whole right side.

What have we got next in stick figures?

Watch the facial expressions.

NOT VERY GOOD! I MUST TRY AND GET A PHOTOGRAPH OF A HURDLER TO LOOK AT.

A GOOD SYMBOL OF BELLS AND WEIRD SOUNDS RINGING IN YOUR HEAD.

41

More stick figures still!

I just tried out the action of a bowler in a bowling alley and it's more like this.

Did this one confuse you?
This is what I imagined in
my mind's eye.

Can you see it now?

43

I started on this drawing of the horse at first, but the reins were too far forward.

The rider would have had to be really thrown forward like this . . . nothing like the original stick figure! Also the horse had all four feet on the ground – I think the action of him kicking was better, but I like the nasty expression on the side view of the horse better. I'll talk more about expressions in a later chapter.

What have we got left from page 15? Ah . . . a baseball player at bat, a pitcher and someone working on a horizontal bar.

Baseball is fairly complicated to draw – especially the pitcher and his wind-up and his throw. I think they are like this.

Well, something like that. The action looks a bit false to me.

The batter makes moves like this . . .

I think I'll leave you to do the chap on the horizontal bar – I'm going to move on to something else.

6
Using models

You should get friends or family to pose for you so you can see how they look doing certain things. Get your Mum and Dad to pretend to be doing things while you try to sketch them.

SOMETHING IN MY EYE!

Your drawing doesn't have to be perfect as long as you capture the important things that convey the movement, the action, the pose.

I've just tried out pulling my lower lid down with my right hand and realised I've got the thumb on the wrong side – it should be like this.

The important thing is, you want people to know from your drawings, what the person in that drawing is doing, *and*, what sort of a person he or she is.

I drew this man who was sitting opposite me in a train – he was half asleep, with legs crossed and one hand tucked inside his coat. I drew him quickly so he wouldn't wake up and get embarrassed or annoyed.

Now, suppose you wanted him to look really cold. How would *you* do it? First, think what things happen to you when you are cold. You shiver, perhaps you grit your teeth and shut your eyes. You pull your coat lapel across your neck to keep warm and bunch up your shoulders . . . but mostly, for the cartoon effect, you need to shiver. Let's try that last man, but now, looking really cold. I've drawn his breath turning to vapour with bits of icicles dripping down from it but most of all – the shivering lines everywhere. O.K.?

If you wanted him as a spy reaching into his inside pocket for a weapon – what would you need to exaggerate? What do you think? Maybe he should have sneaky looking eyes and be wearing a trench coat and a hat.

notice the action highlighted

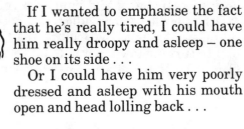

If I wanted to emphasise the fact that he's really tired, I could have him really droopy and asleep – one shoe on its side . . .

Or I could have him very poorly dressed and asleep with his mouth open and head lolling back . . .

No socks, one tooth missing and an unshaven face helps the down-and-out picture. Holes in the boots too, and notice the cartoonist's symbol for snoring – a row of z's.

7
Head proportions

So far I've just been happily drawing away and I've made no mention of proportion. Proportion just means how big one thing is in relation to another thing, and I think correct proportion is something you should know about.

A lot of cartoonists change natural proportions around to get the special sort of shape of person that makes their cartoon unique. So ... if I show you what the normal proportions for features on a human head are, and show you what happens if you *change* those proportions, then your own cartooning will benefit.

First, if you look at a normal head from the side it is roughly this shape.

About halfway between top and bottom are the eyes.

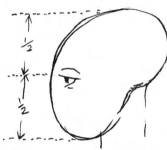

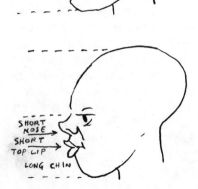

Between the eyes and the chin there are all sorts of possibilities.

The nose may be long or short; the top lip long or short, and each variation changes the way a person looks. The really important measurement to remember is that the eyes are roughly halfway between the chin and the top of the head. The next important measurement is a very hard one to believe. Look . . .

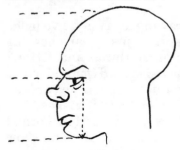

Drop a line from the back corner of the eye straight down to the chin.

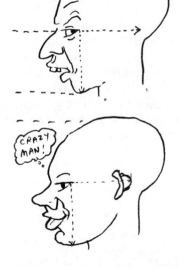

Now, draw a line the same length straight towards the back of the head from that same corner of the eye, and that is where the back of the ear should be.

It really is hard to believe, isn't it?

I'm sure if I'd asked you to position that ear, you would have put it much, much closer to the eye. Am I right?

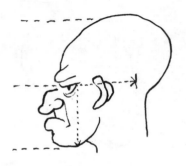

What happens is that when you come to put the ear in its place, there is such a big space between the eye and where the ear should go that your inner self says, 'that is a long boring gap with nothing happening. Let's fill the boring space by putting the ear a bit closer to the eye'.

The same thing tends to happen when you are drawing a face from the front – say you've just drawn the features from chin up to eyes, like this . . .

and you are going to draw up to the hair and the top of the head.

The dotted line shows you roughly where the top of the head *should* be, but this is where most people would draw the top of the head if they didn't measure it first. It doesn't look too bad either . . . does it?

Here's where you should have drawn the hair.

It's the same as it was with positioning the ear on the side view of the face. Your brain sees that big gap from the eyes up to the hair line. It seems to be an awfully boring huge space with nothing happening – so without thinking, you just shorten that gap and put the hair and the top of the head much closer to the eyes.

Of course, there are all sorts of ways that the hair will fit on the head.

And millions more than the three I've drawn . . .

51

Now, take a look at the human head from the *front*. The eyes are halfway up.

As I said, most people drawing a head from the front put the eyes up near the top like this . . .

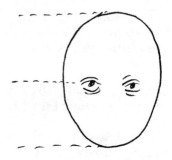

and of course that looks fine in a cartoon, it does look like a happy-go-lucky sort of person. In reality the proportions are more like this.

There are two more little tips on proportion that you should know. First, the ears are usually on a line between the eyes and the nostrils. That is, if you drew dotted lines across at those two points the ears would be between them.

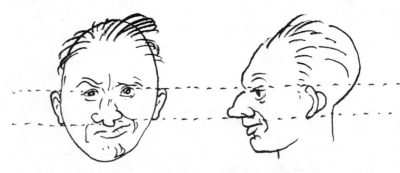

Of course you get people who have abnormally long ears and some who have tiny ears, but that is just a basic rule you can use to give you an idea where the ears should go.

The second tip is this. If you look at a human face from the front, there is usually a space between the eyes about

52

the same size as another eye. If you leave a gap the size of an eye, you won't go far wrong.

Just draw another eye in and you'll see what I mean.

But, of course, all these rules are there to be broken if you want to.

If you have the eyes right up near the top of the head you get these sorts of characters.

They look a bit like you might imagine the village idiot would look . . . not much brain capacity.

If you were to make the distance from the eyes to the top of the head even greater than normal you would get this effect.

Rightly or wrongly you get the feeling they have a large brain capacity and are obviously fairly clever types. This brings up another point: little babies have quite a different proportion from adults.

With young children all the features, eyes, nose, mouth and ears, occupy much less than half the head, and the section from the eyes to the top of the head is much bigger in proportion, much more than half. Also, the eyes seem very big in proportion to everything else.

This is a typical cartoon baby face.

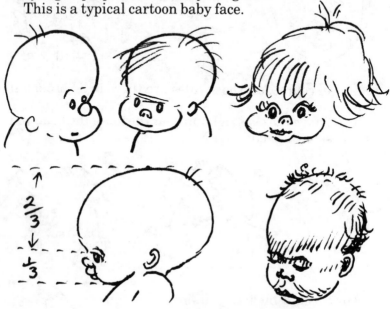

Proportions of actual baby's face from a photograph.

Adults who seem to have those similar proportions are often referred to as 'baby faced'.

So – there you have the basic rules of proportion for the human head. As I've said, all these rules are there to be broken for your own special purpose – but you should know the rules, and what effect you are striving to get when you break them.

8
Hats

In the chapter on posing and characterisation, I drew a hat on the spy character and I wasn't very happy with it. Most people when they start drawing hats find them very difficult. Have a look at some very young children's drawings of hats.

They are delightful drawings but you can see that hats

are a problem. Unless you want to do a hat completely the wrong size for some comic effect – then the actual crown of the hat should be big enough to fit over the top part of the head and when it's on the head, you must be able to imagine the head inside it.

If the hat is supposed to look too small as a joke, then it would sit on top of the head.

But it's no good having the hat too small and fitting like this because the man's head from the top of his brow upwards has to be the right size.

So where does the hat fit? A hat that's too big would slip down and push the ears down too . . . like this . . .

but it's really no good having a hat that is too big, miraculously staying up in the air.

. . .

By rights, that hat should plunge down to here . . .

57

Look at some of the ways hats can be drawn.

9

Human body proportion

Let us look at the body. Most ordinary, non-glamorous people have this sort of shape. If you take the head as a unit of measurement, then most ordinary everyday people would be between four and a half to six heads high – most of them would be about five and a half heads high.

If you know this rule, you can then bend it to suit your own cartoon. In the comic cartoons we see in newspapers or magazines, the head is usually much bigger in proportion to the body, giving you the well-known comic 'little man', or 'little woman'. You know the sort I mean . . .

1 HEAD

2

3

HANDS ALMOST REACH THE KNEES → 4

5

5½

1 HEAD

2

3

3¾ NOTICE THE SHADOW-- SHOWING HE'S OFF THE GROUND AND MOVING.

1 HEAD

1½

If, on the other hand, you want to make your characters statuesque and glamorous, you make them seven and a half to eight and a half heads high. Actors like Charlton Heston have these sorts of proportions. Most of us mere ordinary mortals do not.

So, in contrast to the 'little man' cartoon characters (the ones that we all laugh at and somehow feel superior to), let me show you the proportions of some of the 'hero' characters, the ones we all look up to in awe.

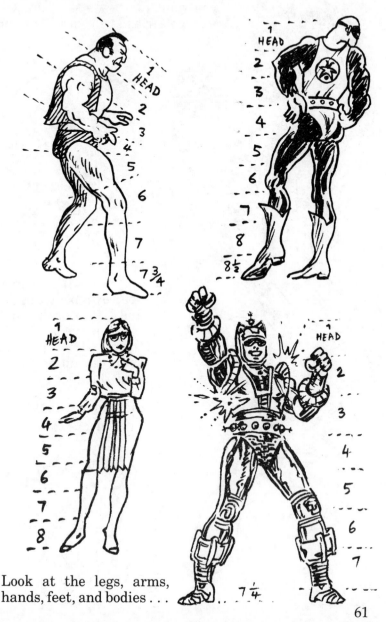

Look at the legs, arms, hands, feet, and bodies . . .

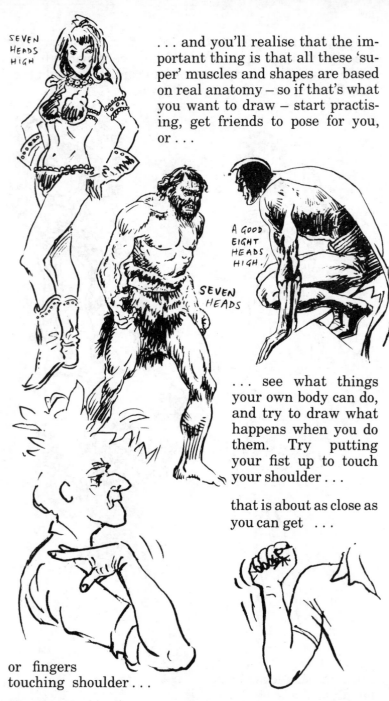

SEVEN
HEADS
HIGH

... and you'll realise that the important thing is that all these 'super' muscles and shapes are based on real anatomy – so if that's what you want to draw – start practising, get friends to pose for you, or ...

A GOOD
EIGHT
HEADS
HIGH.

SEVEN
HEADS

... see what things your own body can do, and try to draw what happens when you do them. Try putting your fist up to touch your shoulder ...

that is about as close as you can get ...

or fingers touching shoulder ...

or arms folded.

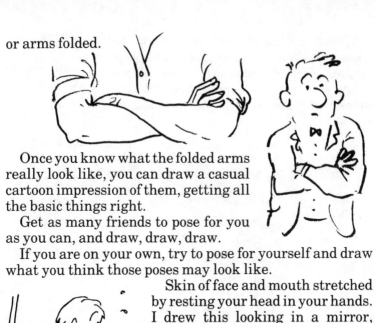

Once you know what the folded arms really look like, you can draw a casual cartoon impression of them, getting all the basic things right.

Get as many friends to pose for you as you can, and draw, draw, draw.

If you are on your own, try to pose for yourself and draw what you think those poses may look like.

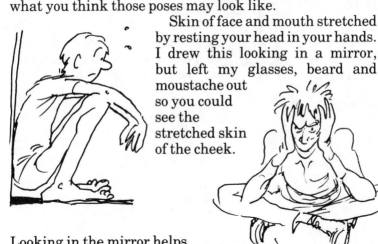

Skin of face and mouth stretched by resting your head in your hands. I drew this looking in a mirror, but left my glasses, beard and moustache out so you could see the stretched skin of the cheek.

Looking in the mirror helps.

IT HASN'T HELPED ME

When you look at the drawings done by someone who hasn't thought about proportions, or perhaps doesn't know about them, you get glaring mistakes – like the arms being too short and only reaching the waist . . .

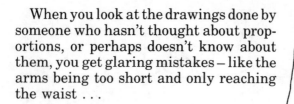

they should be at least to here . . .

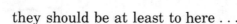

or possibly even longer in some people where you've exaggerated to give an ape-like appearance.

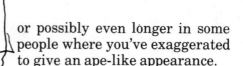

Here are a couple of good rule-of-thumb measurements to remember: the foot, from heel to toe, is about the same length as the inside of the arm from the bend of the elbow to the bend of the wrist.

It's about the same as your hand span too.

Also, the hand, from the heel of the palm to the fingertips is about the same size as the face from chin to hairline. Hard to believe, but just try it with your own hand and face.

So, there you are. The rules of proportion are there to serve you – break them if you wish, to get an effect, but you should be aware that you are breaking the rules and why.

For example . . . if you draw tiny feet or tiny hands, it's either a mistake, or it's being done on purpose to emphasise something in your cartoon.

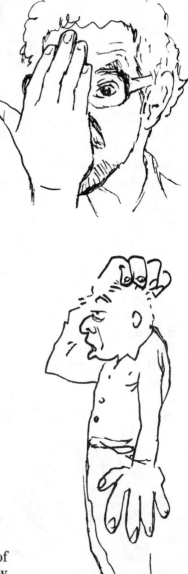

Have a look at the sort of character you get if you draw feet and hands too big. I've just looked at these two *awful* hands I've drawn, and it reminds me that hands and feet are very difficult to draw.

65

10
Hands

Look at the shape of your hand – I'm right-handed, so I'll draw my left hand. (If I wanted to draw what a right hand looked like accurately, I could hold up my left hand and look at it in a mirror.)

My left hand is something like this.

Now, that is a very complicated shape to draw. A tip I was given years ago, was to try to forget the shape of the thumb and the fingers and to draw the shapes of the spaces *between* them. In this way, you are not drawing difficult things that you know, like fingers and thumbs, but rather, just abstract shapes! You have no idea what the shape is *supposed* to look like – so you have more chance of accurately drawing what you see.

Look back at the hand I've just drawn – see the shape

between the thumb and finger. If you draw those shapes accurately, then the *hand* will be right. Let me finish by drawing the two outside chunks of space that come right up to the edge of the hand.

Depending on how well you *see*, and how well you *draw* the surrounding shapes, you will have a pretty good hand revealed by the edges of those shapes.

If you want to simplify a hand – look at your own – could you organise some shapes you might be able to draw quickly?

Try a circle . . . now about a third of the way down, draw the crease across – then two fingers one taller than the other.

Add the next two and a thumb.
Does this help?

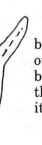

Don't forget that the hand has a bunch of bones inside radiating out from the wrist, so if you can bear that in mind when drawing the front or back view of the hand, it helps.

LEFT HAND IN THE MIRROR

Look at the different ways the fingers can team up together.

67

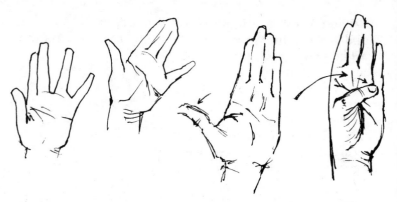

Look too at the ways the hand can bend and fold up

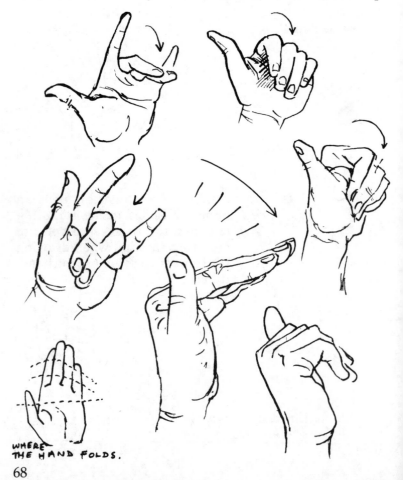

WHERE
THE HAND FOLDS.

Look at the way cartoonists draw hands and the ways in which they simplify those hands. Here are as many hands as I can think of.

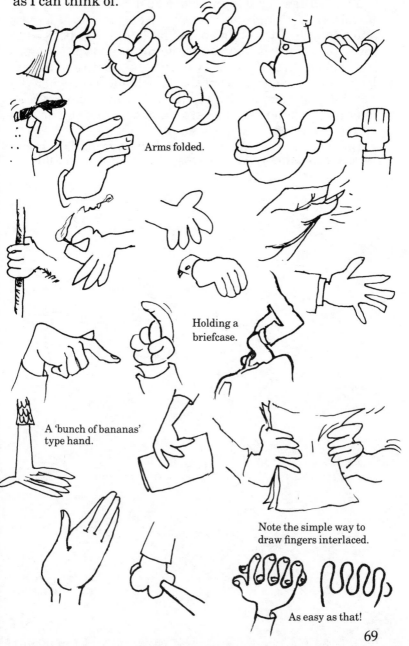

Arms folded.

Holding a briefcase.

A 'bunch of bananas' type hand.

Note the simple way to draw fingers interlaced.

As easy as that!

Do you notice anything strange? Just check the number of fingers on each of those hands.

You will see that some cartoon hands have got four fingers and a thumb, and some have only got three fingers and a thumb. I'll explain about that later in the book – the important thing is, the hand is doing 'hand-type' things – it is folding up in the right way and the thumb and fingers look roughly 'right' in what they are doing. Even when the hand is just sloppily drawn like a bunch of bananas, as long as the action of the cartoon gets across to you, the reader, then that drawing works!

Did you notice there were very few fingernails? I guess they are an added complication.

11
Feet

Feet are just as difficult as hands to draw. I've just taken my shoes and socks off and here's roughly what my feet look like in repose.

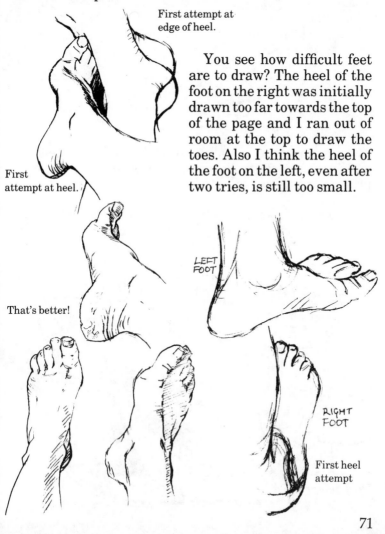

First attempt at edge of heel.

You see how difficult feet are to draw? The heel of the foot on the right was initially drawn too far towards the top of the page and I ran out of room at the top to draw the toes. Also I think the heel of the foot on the left, even after two tries, is still too small.

First attempt at heel.

That's better!

LEFT FOOT

RIGHT FOOT

First heel attempt

I'll do some drawings of someone else's foot, then I can get a more side-on viewpoint.

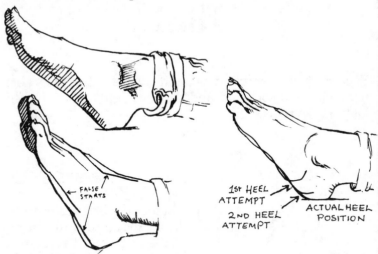

FALSE STARTS

1ST HEEL ATTEMPT

2ND HEEL ATTEMPT

ACTUAL HEEL POSITION

There's no shame in making mistakes. Some of Leonardo da Vinci's drawings show two or three attempts to get the proportions right.

Let me have a look at some cartoon feet from the 'little man' type of comic strips. Here are as many as I can think of.

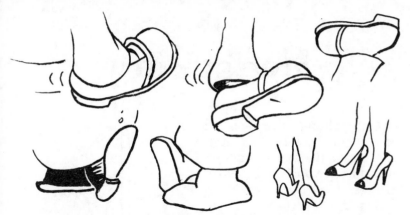

A lot of comic cartoon strips never go below waist level, so they never get to the problem of drawing feet at all. As you can see, with bare feet, or feet with shoes on, the strip cartoonist does the simplest job he can, to show that the person has the weight firmly resting on those feet. In this sort of cartooning, the shape of foot and toe need bear no relation to what feet really look like – as long as you can understand what the action is – that's the important thing!

In the larger-than-life hero type cartoons the feet are beautifully drawn once again – here are some such feet.

12.
Measuring

Quite often as I've been talking about drawing I've said 'I
measured it', and I thought I
should tell you how I measure
things.

Try this.

Hold your pencil in this grip
and the fourth finger will quite
naturally hold the pencil upright.

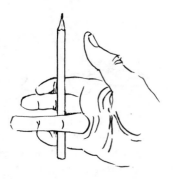

Now, extend the hand to
the full length of the arm
keeping the pencil vertical –
use the very point of the pencil as one end of whatever
you want to measure and use
the thumb nail to slide up or
down the pencil to position
accurately the other end of
what you're measuring.

In this case I'm measuring
the boy's head from the top of
the head to the chin. As you
can see, it is quite easy to
turn the hand to hold the
pencil in a horizontal position if you wanted to see how
wide his head was.

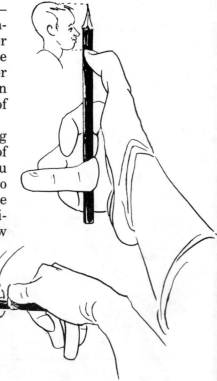

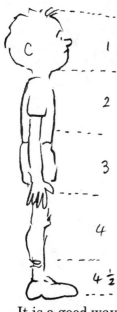

Here is a way you might use measurement of this kind.

Say you wanted to see how tall the boy was. You could just check off the size of his head with your eye and your 'pencil and thumb' measurement, and see how many of these measures it takes to fit into the whole body height. Then if you wished, you could pin-point where each measure fitted. For example, the second one is about at his elbow and just above the waist of the shorts, the third one is right at his thumb, the fourth at his socks.

See how it works?

It is a good way to see if you've got your drawing in the right proportion. For example – how long is a hand compared to its width? You just take a 'thumb to the tip of the pencil' measurement of the width of the hand – then you swivel the measuring hand round so the pencil is horizontal and you check off that measurement against the length and you find that it is nearly two of those measures from the 'heel' of the hand to the tip of the longest finger.

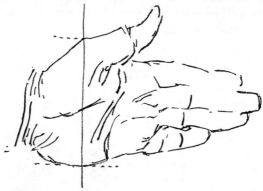

It just gives you a check on your drawing – you can compare length of nose to length of ear, chin to eyes, and eyes to the top of the head etc.

Here's another example. You are drawing someone and you've got down to the feet. Now, how big should the feet be? Remember that earlier I said a foot is roughly the same length as the inside of the elbow to the bend of the wrist? Right! Measure that with your pencil – either from the subject you are drawing, or from your partly completed drawing, and there's your foot length. Swivel your hand round and mark it off on the paper, then you have a fairly accurate length for your foot (near enough for a cartoon anyway!).

I hope that's fairly clear. It's good to measure using the sharpened end of the pencil because then you can just do a little pencil line with the tip of the pencil at each measurement on your paper.

13

Different viewpoints

You will notice in some comic strips that the artist has changed the viewpoint. He may draw one picture as if seen from the floor and in the next, the view will be from one corner of the ceiling, and so on. This stops the strip from getting boring. Here are a few examples picked out of comic strips.

See the two different points of view in these consecutive pictures, then you get a picture from the level of the pavement, which is a slightly tilted pavement.

Have a look at this next picture. It is obviously on board a ship and drawn from a viewpoint overhead in the rigging.

Now ... if *you* are going to be changing the angle of viewpoint it is going to give you problems because a face looks totally different when seen from above, from below, from the front, from the side, or from any spot halfway between.

How do you go about drawing heads from any of these different angles?

Well, imagine a very simplified face drawn on a rugby ball shape. Stick a couple of ears on and draw dotted lines to mark the line of the eyes, the nose and the mouth.

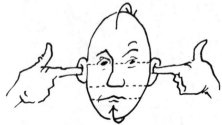

Imagine you stick one index finger in each ear so that you can gently rotate the head in the direction of the arrows.

(That is, the chin moves forward and the top of the head moves back.)

Right. Do it!

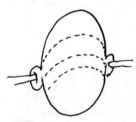

Straightaway you see the dotted lines for eyes, nose and mouth have moved.

Draw the eyes, nose and mouth in their new positions.

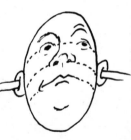

Rotate it even further and it would look like this.

If you rotated it downwards, the dotted lines for the nose, mouth and eyes would curve the other way, like this.

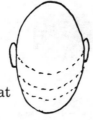

Add the features to that shape and you have this.

If you tilt it further and further in the downwards direction you would get these head shapes.

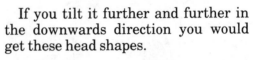

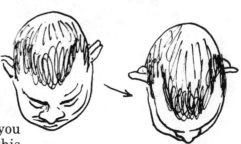

The best way for you to do drawings like this is to get someone to pose for you. Of course, if you do get

someone to tilt their head back and you look up at them from underneath, there's all that bulgy bit of the Adam's apple that wasn't on the rugby ball model. You will also see lots of hair at the bottom on both sides of the neck.

It looks something like this.

See how many faces you can find from cartoons where they are drawn from fancy angles, over the shoulder, from above, from below, from the floor or from the ceiling.

They don't usually occur in the 'little man' comedy strips, more in the larger-than-life 'hero' type comics.

Here are a few I've copied from various comic books and strips.

You can rotate the rugby ball to the side to work out what a side-view of a head would look like. Do a dotted line down the centre of the ball – as the ball turns, so that dotted line turns like this . . .

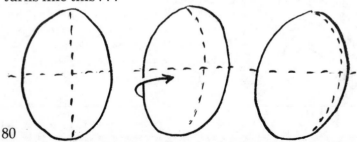

giving you features like this.

The only problem here is that a head seen from the side is *not* like a rugby ball. The head has a second bulky curved shape at the back – imagine another rugby ball drawn horizontally at the top like this.

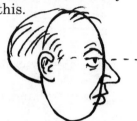

That is more or less what a head looks like from the side, in a very simplified way.

If you add the neck to support that, you have a basic head shape.

You can, of course, tilt *and* turn so that you get all sorts of combinations of angles, as in page 79.

14

Foreshortening

Imagine a person falling towards you like this.

Now . . . what will the viewer see?

Notice the dotted lines from the eye of the viewer to the 'tripper'.

The closest thing to you, the viewer, is the front hand. It will look bigger because it is closer.

Next, the face and the other hand are roughly the same distance from your eye, so they will be about the same size as each other, but smaller than the front hand. So it goes on . . . the bent knee is next, and then furthest away is the foot doing the tripping.

If you were to draw the 'tripper' from your front-on view, it might look like this.

Foreshortening is very difficult, and any time you want to do any drawings using it, it's best to get someone to pose for you.

I've just got a friend to lie on his stomach over the end of a settee with both hands up and you can see how different the hand and arm shapes are from what I imagined they would be.

The actual *sizes* of the hands, however, demonstrate the foreshortening perfectly. Look at some drawings of foreshortening from comic strips.

LYING DOWN WITH ONE ARM OUTSTRETCHED

ALMOST THE SAME AS THE "TRIPPER"

ONE FORE-SHORTENED LEG

(GOOD RUNNING ACTION!)

MAN COMING STRAIGHT UP TOWARDS YOU.

15

Lop-sided faces

If you drew anybody's face really accurately from the front, and you then ruled a line right down through the centre of the nose, you would find that the two sides of the face are totally different to one another. They are *not* symmetrical.

Even when I'm *trying* to draw both sides of a face exactly the same, I find it difficult.

Let me draw myself in a mirror and you'll see what I mean.

This is roughly how I see myself in the mirror.

I've turned that drawing back to front and traced it. This is how the camera sees me.

It's also how you would see me if you met me face to face. I don't recognise myself in a photo because I am used to seeing my mirror image – and that is quite different to a photograph. I am used to seeing that heavy smile line on the *left-hand* side of my face in the mirror and the slightly raised eyebrow, just sticking out over the *right-hand* lens of my glasses. The camera sees it exactly the other way round.

Let me split the photographed face down the middle of the nose with a straight line, as I described at the beginning of this section.

As you can see – the sides *are* different. A dramatic way of demonstrating this difference is to draw the left side – then turn the paper over and trace another left side as the other half of the face, then repeat this process with two right sides of the face.

LEFT
SIDE

LEFT
SIDE
REVERSED

REVERSED
RIGHT
SIDE

RIGHT
SIDE

In nature, faces are *not* symmetrical. Most people smile much more heavily on one side than the other. Eyebrows are higher one side than the other. This is an important thing to remember when you are drawing faces from the front. If you are drawing pictures of yourself or friends, look for the lop-sidedness in a face and exaggerate it. If you are making up faces, bear it in mind and try and make sure those faces are a bit lop-sided. It will make your drawings more real. I'll just make up a few faces.

With some people, one eye is lower than the other.

One lazy eyelid.   These three are from photographs.

Here are some more drawn from photographs. See how uneven the two sides of the faces are.

Not many wrinkles yet in the young man's face, but you can see the lop-sided mouth, nose and eyes.

In cartoon books and comic strips, you don't see too much lop-sidedness, but it is there if you look for it.

86

16

Characteristics

If you want to draw a person with certain characteristics, there are a lot of face shapes which are immediately recognisable as certain types of people to the ordinary reader.

Look at these faces and guess what sort of people they are. What do they do for a living?

BOXER ? TOUGH GUY ?

UNTRUSTWORTHY CON - MAN ?

A BIT SIMPLE ?

A TWIT ?

NOT GETTING ENOUGH SLEEP ?

A FLIRT ?

NOT SURE OF HIM. A JOKER?

MONKEY FACE ?

"SEEN IT ALL BEFORE" TYPE.

And so it goes on. You can pick up lots of different features, and put them together to create all sorts of characters.

17

Expressions

I just looked at that last page and realised the 'what have I done' and the 'what do I do now' characters are not so much different 'types' but rather have different facial expressions, drawn to convey certain moods.

Stand in front of a mirror and pull faces to show certain emotions and see if you can draw those faces simply like this

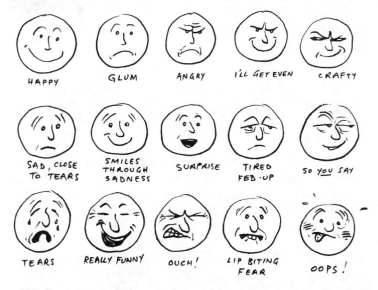

HAPPY   GLUM   ANGRY   I'LL GET EVEN   CRAFTY

SAD, CLOSE TO TEARS   SMILES THROUGH SADNESS   SURPRISE   TIRED FED-UP   SO YOU SAY

TEARS   REALLY FUNNY   OUCH!   LIP BITING FEAR   OOPS!

With a young person's face, there are very few lines or wrinkles, so if you are a youngster drawing your mirror image, you'll just have to guess where the lines will appear. The main lines that can help you to indicate expressions are, first the mouthshape, then the line from the nostril down to the corner of the mouth, third, the eyebrow position, and fourth, the wrinkles above the eyebrow. Little 'crow's feet' appear at the outside corners of the eyes when you crinkle them up in laughter, or against fierce sunlight.

The eyes themselves can show a lot of expressions – as follows . . .

but then of course, you can put those eyes with different mouth and eyebrow shapes and you can get all sorts of unexpected expressions.

After doing all sorts of drawings of yourself in the mirror, you can actually close your eyes and imagine what creases and lines will appear to create certain expressions.

Draw someone slowly starting to smile.

Try someone starting to look sideways and frowning.

You will also find that you can make that expression look even more positive if you include some body positions as well as the face.

If you wanted to show someone who was almost asleep but desperately trying to keep his or her eyes open by raising the eyebrows, it could be like this.

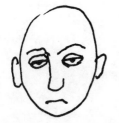

When the eyebrows are raised, the eyes still look sleepy. (Note wrinkles on forehead.)

The position of the shoulders gives a good indication of a person's feelings – check these poses.

Note movement of Adam's apple – nervous swallowing.

Upset.

With the same face expression, this one looks apprehensive.

This one looks worried sick.

Self satisfied, rocking on his heels.

Scared silly.

18

Animals as cartoon characters

When the first animators were faced with making moving pictures of cartoon characters, they had all sorts of problems. The main problem was that they had about 25 pictures projected on to the screen every second.

Think about that . . . EVERY SECOND!

That means that a five-minute cartoon would have over seven *thousand* individual and different pictures. These had to be photographed, and before they were photographed, they had to be drawn, and then inked in.

In later years colour was an added complication – but let's go back to the 'black and white' days. Imagine how many different people with different talents and abilities would be working on the drawings during the making of a cartoon film.

The problems were solved by simplifying the characters, by basing them on shapes that everyone can draw. The features of face and body were simplified and all the different expressions were drawn from every possible angle so that a complete set of reference pictures was always available.

Take a dog for example. Imagine you wanted to make a cartoon about this one.

How are you going to approach it?

You could attempt a realistic drawing of the dog with a body shape like this.

The problem is that this character is limited to doing only dog-type things.

He couldn't get involved in a plot where he had to pick up a dish with his hand, for example.

You could make the character part-human, with arms and hands instead of front legs and paws, and you could have him standing upright instead of on all-fours.

He might look like this.

Or you might draw his hind legs so that they actually bend like a human's legs and you may even dress the character in clothes so that he is always recognisable by his face AND by what he wears.

Perhaps a hat with his name on would help too . . .

Then of course you must start to think about facial expressions.

Look at this dog's face.

He is actually fairly relaxed – probably hot and possibly panting after a long run somewhere. If you tried to relate his face to what you know of human expressions, you may imagine him as very happy and perhaps laughing uproariously at a joke.

When we are told someone is very angry we imagine them to be frowning with their brow all creased, with frown lines and eyes almost hidden by eyebrows, and a down-turned corner of the mouth – perhaps hunched shoulders. Look at yourself in the mirror and pull an angry face.

That sort of look says 'very angry, possibly planning an attack'.

Now if a dog is angry and is planning to attack someone, he doesn't frown at all. First his hackles rise – that is, all the hair around the back of his neck and shoulders stands on end. And secondly, he pulls his lips back to reveal all his teeth and he gives a menacing growl.

So, most people watching a cartoon, unless they knew a lot about dogs, would not recognise a dog doing those things as being an angry dog. They would expect to see him frowning and turning down the corners of his mouth, and perhaps hunching his shoulders and bunching his 'hands' up into aggressive-looking fists.

This is what they would recognise as 'angry'.

Take a cat as another example. The nearest thing to smiling in a cat's body language would be when the cat is totally at ease and not expecting any attack. Then it would feel confident and relaxed enough to actually close its eyes. This is how you know when a cat is happy and contented.

A HAPPY RELAXED CAT

When a cat is angry or ready for a fight, its ears go down flat out of harm's way and its eyes open as wide as possible to make sure it sees as clearly as possible any attack that may come.

A CAT YAWNING

The fur often stands on end to make the cat look bigger and more frightening to an enemy. The cat may even open its mouth and do that hissing spitting thing cats do.

AN ANGRY CAT SPITTING

If we relate these three pictures to what we know of human facial reactions, we may think the first one is either bored stupid, or has just stood on a nail and is being strong and silent while actually in pain.

The second could be laughing at a joke. The third one may be like a shy demure girl, surprised and delighted at an unexpected gift.

So you see, for the cartoons, it was decided to combine characteristic animal reactions and movements, with all the smiles, frowns, worry wrinkles, eyebrow movements and open-mouthed laughs of the human being – letting the audience know instantly what emotion was being shown on the screen.

All these things, of course, a cat would never do, but people recognise the human counterpart.

Look at these cat faces with human-type eyes:

Immediately you try to draw these human expressions on a cat's face you realise the limitations of that typical cat-shaped mouth. Somehow – whatever other expression you put on the rest of the face – that mouth always seems to us to be smiling. How much better for the expression if the cartoonist ignored that part of the cat and made the mouth a more human shape. Then you could

really start to get human-looking expressions on the face.

People can recognise the expressions much more easily when eyes and mouth are more like the human counterpart. The nose and the ears are not as important in human expressions so the cartoonist could virtually do any old thing he liked with them.

Going back to our original dog character, we would really need to change his eyes from little buttons into ones where we could see the whites of the eyes better.

A small white eyebrow in the black patch will also help.

Now – you can start to get some expressions that we can all recognise:

Imagine what he would look like from the side.

As you see, I've changed his hands to three fingers and a thumb – and I've also put gloves on them.

Most cartoonists drew three-fingered hands, because they were less complicated to draw than four fingers, and with gloves on, all the complicated creases that occur in the skin of a hand are hidden. And on top of that, you don't need to draw fingernails . . . much simpler!

You could of course go back to a character without clothes and with doggy-type hind legs.

In fact, you can draw whatever you want to!

All the cartoon animal characters you see are based on their real animal counterpart. If you wanted to draw a duck-type character, for example, you could go back to nature (as in fact the early cartoonists did) and try to simplify slightly what you see.

Take a very elegant bird, the pintail drake, as an example. His front part looks something like this.

If you were to try to make a cartoon character of this fellow – how would you go about it? You want to keep his bill the same shape . . . maybe exagerrate it a bit – like this:

You could move his eyes from the sides of his head to the front, so they look a bit more like human's eyes.

Try this.

I've added a tiny bump at the corner of the mouth to indicate a human type smile, and also two suggestions of tiny eyebrows over the eyes.

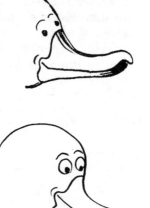

Let's try to make his eyes a bit bigger and we'll include some whites of eyes as well as eyebrows.

You could give him a special hairdo, so you'd know him anywhere (and I've enlarged the eyes, *and* put a little bit of a frown on one eyebrow).

Do we want this character to do duck-type things . . . or do we want him to be able to grab things and hold them?

I've made the head a bit small for the body, haven't I?

If he's going to hold things, we need arms instead of wings.

What sort of body could we design to take in his arms?

Don't like the neck much.

As we make the body smaller, the character gets more appealing.

We could remove the neck and give him big shoulders.

You can do whatever you want with your characters.

Imagine if you put arms on the original duck – how would that look?

It doesn't look very good, does it? If we just drew a little man and put a duck's head, feet and tail feathers on, how would that look?

You really can do anything you want to do. Here's a tip for making the eyes look really good. Have a look at the heads of those last three. The eye on the head on the right looks alive as opposed to the dead dull black eyes on the other two heads.

The difference is the point of light in the eye on the right. When I'm drawing eyes I usually leave a little light in the middle.

Eyes are beautifully wet, shiny, curved, reflecting surfaces and will pick up pin-points of light from any light bulb or flashlight or burst of sunshine.

In the early film cartoon characters there was no light in

the eyes, but in later cartoons the light was drawn as a sharp triangle of white 'nicked' out of the black part of each eye, like a wedge cut out of a round cheese.

Look how alive those eyes look.

In some cartoons the pupil of the eye is outlined around the light – like this.

Some cartoons even have the triangle of light outlined across the whole of the eye – like this.

I like the first one best and the last one not at all. How about you?

It's really a lot easier just to leave a spot of light in the eye as you draw it. It's fairly important that the spot of light is in the same relative position in each of a character's two eyes.

 THIS NOT THIS

If an eyelid is half-closed it may block off the light.

Something I just thought of, which you may not realise.

If you're right-handed, you usually prefer to draw people facing to the left, because then all the curves of the forehead and so on all go the way your hand draws most easily,

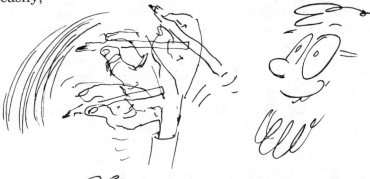

whereas, a face looking the other way is awkward to draw because the right-hand movement doesn't flow on these curves.

See how stilted it looks!

If you're left-handed it's the reverse of course.

O.K. – back to animals as cartoon characters.

I said earlier on that a nose and ears don't do much towards altering a human's expression, so it doesn't matter what you do with them. In most animals, however, a changing ear position alters the expression enormously –

take these two dogs for example. Check the different expressions.

In certain animals, where ears are large and very important, their position could do a lot towards altering the expression of any cartoon version you might draw.

Take a koala from Australia. The typical face shape of a koala is like this.

Without altering anything you can relate that face to a human face and start to put human expressions onto it.

Notice how much better those first two expressions would be if you moved the ears. Drooping ears help that hang-dog look, and perked-up, alert ears work really well for an excited 'what's going on?' look.

Take an animal like a rabbit, for example, which has very large ears. Different ear shapes and positions could do a lot to change his expression.

There is something tremendously appealing to most of us in a baby, a baby of any sort – baby duck, baby human, baby elephant – our reaction is 'Ah . . .'.

It's the same in cartoons. I've dealt with babies' facial proportions earlier (page 54) and they really apply to a baby of any sort.

First, and most important, is that the features, nose, mouth, eyes and eyebrows, occupy a very small portion of the whole head – probably about one-third. The eyes are usually very large and sometimes look slightly cross-eyed. No lines or wrinkles have appeared as yet.

Imagine a cartoon about koalas.

With an adult koala's face you would have the eyes about half-way up to the top of the head, indicating ordinary grown-up proportions.

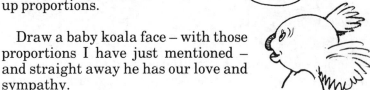

Draw a baby koala face – with those proportions I have just mentioned – and straight away he has our love and sympathy.

We were talking about baby animals being appealing. Look at this puppy:

His face has great charm, hasn't it?

There are so many different breeds of dog that you could almost get any type of character you wanted by drawing different breeds.

You could draw the big aggressive bruiser character as a cartoon bulldog – big jaw, bad-tempered eyebrows frowning, small brain capacity, big chest.

You could have a grey-hound as a sort of scared, timid type with a few shaking lines around him.

There are not so many different faces to choose from with cats – but here are a few.

Try to draw your own style of cat. Look at a cat's face. What do you think are the important features?

Here's what a British Blue looks like

A tabby cat.

A cat yawning.

As you can see, a real cat has some very important features which the animated cartoon cats never even touch on – probably these features would take away from their recognisable 'human' characteristics – things like the horizontal lines of dots across their cheeks where the whiskers spring from – the vertical line of the pupil in the eye, and this important shape of the mouth just below the nose.

 Cartoon eyes always seem to be this shape. whereas in reality the cat's eyes would be more this shape.

Anyway . . . go back to nature – see what you think are the important things about a cat and then look at some of your own expressions in a mirror and see if you can do some funny human-type expressions for *your* cat. Look at your eyes and mouth when you're looking worried, annoyed, afraid, sneaky.

Would this be your cat?

Or this?

This?

Or this?

When I was a youngster I used to draw cats from the back – like this.

Have fun with your cat drawings!

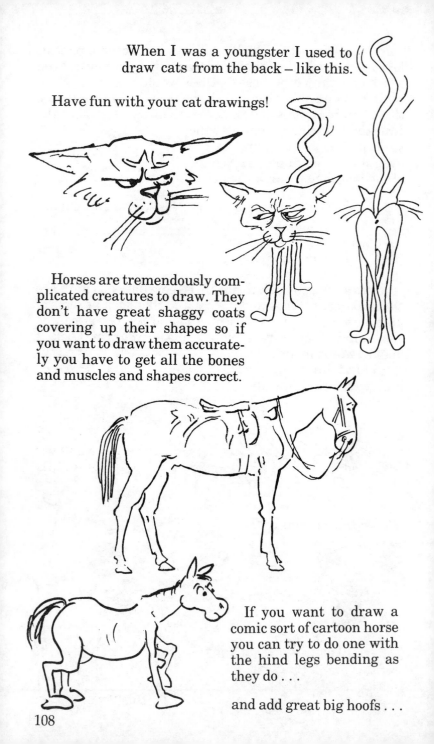

Horses are tremendously complicated creatures to draw. They don't have great shaggy coats covering up their shapes so if you want to draw them accurately you have to get all the bones and muscles and shapes correct.

If you want to draw a comic sort of cartoon horse you can try to do one with the hind legs bending as they do . . .

and add great big hoofs . . .

Or you could do a character created out of circles:

You could even do the legs all bending the same way like this:

The hind legs don't look too good do they?

Mostly when animals walk their limbs move like a human's, insofar as the right foreleg will be moving forward as the right hind leg is moving back like this:

Some animals have been taught to walk with the right foreleg and the right hind leg moving forward as the left legs move back. I think this is called 'pacing' but whatever it's called, it looks a bit awkward to me, even if the animal is doing it naturally.

Just make sure you get the feeling right . . .

and the drawing will work even if the anatomy is completely wrong!

19
Captions

If you are drawing a cartoon and you want one of the characters to be saying something then you need to use what is commonly called a speech 'balloon'.

WHY IS IT OBVIOUS?

WHO'S CLEVER THEN?

There are some traps. For example, always write out the words first – *then* you can fit the balloon around them.

If you draw the balloon in first – you might not be able to fit all the words in.

GOOD GRIEF! I DON'T THINK I'VE GOT ROOM FOR ALL THE WORDS.

I WAS CLEVER. I PLANNED IT SO THAT THE WORDS WOULD FIT!

Another mistake is to have your captions in the wrong place – so that the speech between two people doesn't flow from left to right, the way we're all taught to read.

JUST DOWN TO THE CORNER.

WHERE ARE YOU GOING?

There are two ways of fixing up that situation. The most obvious one is to re-draw the picture with the one who is speaking first on the left-hand side of the picture so that the two speech balloons read correctly from left to right.

The other way to fix it would be to have the speech balloons one above the other, like this.

In some cartoons you see very complicated conversations taking place between two characters using this technique of speech balloons one above the other, like this.

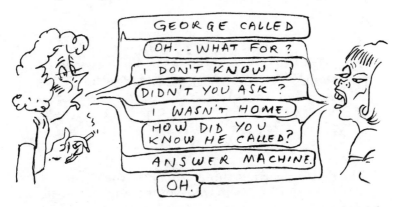

They make the speech balloon a bit tidier than that . . . but that's the rough idea.

Another way of getting the story across is to use 'think' captions. Instead of having the balloon on a bit of string, as it were, you put a set of little bubbles coming from the back of the head (or from wherever you imagine that character is thinking).

You can, of course, combine speech and 'think' balloons.

The most important thing is to make the message clear and get the joke across to whoever is going to look at your cartoon.

Instead of using speech balloons you can print the speech under the cartoon – like this:

"SORRY TO HAVE BEEN SO LONG – THANKS FOR WAITING .... OKAY .. WHENEVER YOU LIKE."

In this sort of cartoon you've got to make sure only one person in the drawing has his mouth open otherwise there will be confusion as to who is saying what.

Have a look at this cartoon as an example.

"WANTING TO SEE THE DOCTOR OR THE DENTIST?"

In this case everybody's mouth is open and anyone could be saying that line – very confusing.

If you have the wrong person with the mouth open the cartoon just doesn't work at all. Look at this one.

"AND WHAT IS YOUR COUNTRY OF ORIGIN?"

In this case it should have been the immigration officer with his mouth open and the Scot looking amazed but with his mouth closed.

This would have been better.

"WHAT IS YOUR COUNTRY OF ORIGIN?"

Just make sure that your cartoon leaves no doubt as to who says what.

20

Inspiration

People are always asking me "Where do you get your ideas from?"

It's something I've never thought about much – one of the first drawings I ever did was of my Father running late for the train – I was about four I think, but I can remember it still. – He had a huge watch in his hand and I ran out of space at the top right hand corner of the page so his neck bent at a really weird angle to fit his head in.

"Taboo" things are always fascinating to draw – I got into real trouble when I was about five for drawing a man with no clothes on having a "wee". The thing that made it really funny for me was that he had urinated so much it was already up around his ankles! He was standing in a vast sea of it . . . most amusing!

It was anatomically very good too – I got a good old spanking for that I seem to recall. Parents were very "victorian" in those days.

Anyway – your inspiration should come from the things around you . . . the things you know.

Any incidents which cause a lot of fun and laughter in your family or amongst friends are ideal. See if you can work out why it was so funny and get the whole incident down on paper. It doesn't have to be perfect – try and get the action – gran's wheelchair wheel flattened the cat's tail and the squawk from the cat made someone drop something . . . DRAW IT!

See if you can get some of the features right – what does the milkman look like? Thin? Fat? Short? Tall? Mustache? Is the cat black with white socks etc. etc.

Everyone in the family will remember the incident and if you have the action right – or even a bit exaggerated it will be a huge success.

Try drawing some funny things that have happened to you – things that maybe only your own family will laugh at – perhaps because they know the person or the people involved.

This is one from my own experience.

What is it that makes a joke? It's usually seeing something happening to someone else and you laugh because you're so relieved it isn't happening to you. The old banana skin joke is a case in point.

Try to think of incidents that were accidental, but are very funny when you look back at them.

Can you see what's going to happen?

Yes . . . you were right! That actually happened to a friend of mine who was visiting relatives in Canada. She had a black eye that you wouldn't believe for about a month – very painful at the time – but looking back it could be something which amuses people.

Does that strike you as funny?

What about this one?

Have *you* ever done something as embarrassing as that?

Draw it! Have a laugh at yourself.

Perhaps I should have made that last one a two picture cartoon. Would it have been better with a picture like this first?

Maybe it would have been better in darkness so you get the idea Father has been woken at the dead of night.

Would it have been better still with a black background! – Really night time!

21
Make the most of your skills

Let's consider some things you can do with your drawings. You can make your own simple movie cartoons. Try this – it's magical!

Get a piece of fairly good notepaper – cut or carefully tear off a piece which is about six times as long as it is wide.

A really good way to tear paper accurately is to fold it and crease it down sharply with a finger nail. Then (and this is the secret bit), just run your tongue along that crease so that you moisten the paper slightly all the way along – allow a few seconds so that the moisture can get into the paper properly, then tear the paper in the normal way – supporting the paper with your other hand. The dampness softens the fibres of the paper and it rips beautifully.

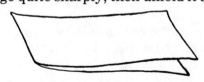

Back to our homemade movie. Fold your paper in half. Crease the edge quite sharply, then unfold it again.

Now, on the centre third of the right-hand half of the paper draw a side view of a face with mouth closed, eyebrows raised, and perhaps a single hair growing luxuriantly on top.

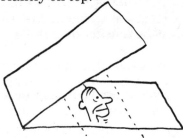

Now ... fold the paper back in half and you should be able to see very faintly, the face that you drew through the top half of the paper. If you can't see it, put your folded paper on a window pane so the daylight shines through.

The secret is to trace exactly the parts of the face that will remain the same, and re-draw, in a new position, the parts of the face that are to move, in this case, the mouth and the chin, the eyebrows and the hair.

The next step is to roll the top piece over a pencil so that it becomes a tightly coiled spring like this.

Then, if you hold the drawing down at point X with the index finger of the left hand, insert a pencil into the spring and move the pencil to the right until the top picture is revealed and then back so that the bottom picture reappears (and so on, over and over again) the face appears to move in a really lifelike way.

Every time the 'mouth open' picture appears you can do a comedy voice sound effect shouting 'no!' to add even more realism to it all. Great fun!

If you move it too fast the illusion of a movie cartoon is lost.

Let me just suggest that you do the passive drawing first on the bottom picture and the one where the action takes place on the top picture. If there is any movement, it is best if it is from left to right, the way the top section unrolls.

Here are a series of 'one, two' type repeating actions that I have found to be most effective – you can see which bits need to be traced accurately and which bits need to be re-drawn.

I'll draw the bottom drawing on the left-hand side and the top drawing on the right in each case.

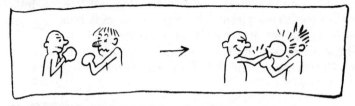

You can draw those little visual 'echoes' to show where the moving part has been.

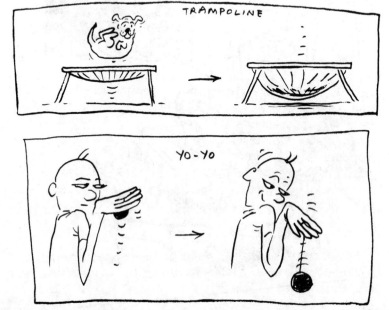

You can get endless fun out of drawing and operating these simple 'reciprocal' movies. Make up some of your own.

Your own Christmas cards are good to do, because then they become personal, and you can do some special lettering and address them by name to special people – then there is no other Christmas card or Birthday card (or whatever type of card it is) like it in the world. Here are a few Christmas cards that I have done over the years.

And here's one made by my daughter when she was very young, showing her greeting the postman on Christmas day, with Mummy and Daddy looking on.

125

I did most of mine by making lino cuts and printing them, but that is a laborious process and if you want to send out lots of cards, you can get a printer to make a block from your drawing and print off a couple of hundred. This will, of course, cost money, so if you are planning to make your own printing block by hand, remember that all lettering comes out in reverse when you print it – that means you have to cut the letters in reverse to have them print right.

Imagine the problems I had making these complicated lino cuts.

Making birthday cards or specialised get well cards is a lovely thing to do.

If your friend is in plaster with a broken leg you could do a simple drawing with a bit of comedy in it.

The 'get well soon' lettering is in a style of block letters. I use this a lot, but you will want to work out which lettering you like to do best. The easiest pens to use for lettering are the ones with a chisel point. With these you can get thick strokes and thin strokes on lettering.

The key to good printing is practice, practice, practice, and a good way to practise lettering is on newspapers. They have plenty of horizontal lines of print and verticals so using a big felt marker pen you can use up as much paper as you like and still have guide lines to keep your letters straight.

You can if you wish draw pencil lines across as a guide, and then just practise the capitals A B C etc. Get nice straight verticals, and try to get the spacing between letters to work – you need less space between curved letters and a bit more between parallel letters like I H N and L.

Once you have mastered basic lettering you can start developing your own style of lettering with a bit of humour in it perhaps.

The important thing to remember is that you *must* be able to read it.

Lettering which gets so 'cute' that you don't actually know what the words are, is bad lettering.

Here is the worst lettering I ever saw on a building. *Everything* is wrong!

It is so hard to read that it took me all my time to decide it was "FATSO". The most important thing about lettering is that it should be easy to read, and all those decorations across the letters of "FATSO" just confuse everthing.

If you want to do shadows on letters they should all be behind all of the letters, not in front of some of them. Also the shading should all go the same way.

This would work:

One has learned from childhood to read letters flowing in a certain direction and so when words are written in a different direction they become almost unrecognisable.

Look at this:

SANDWICHES

PIES

You *can* eventually work it out, but we have been used to seeing it written from left to right all our lives. Don't print words in a confusing or unrecognisable way if you want them to be understood.

AND

Some decoration can be interesting and raise a smile like this one –

but the important thing is . . . you must be able to read the word easily.

If you have done a drawing and you are going to add lettering, it's a good idea to do a trial run on a scrap of paper or tracing paper so that you can get the spacing and the layout looking good.

On any sort of card you need space all around the border and usually a little bit more along the bottom than elsewhere.

You can use lettering, cartoons, pasted-on pictures even . . . in fact anything, to make your own personalised cards.

To make them really unique include the name of the person, the date, and the occasion (wedding aniversary, birthday etc) on each card, and also your own special 'logo' on the back.

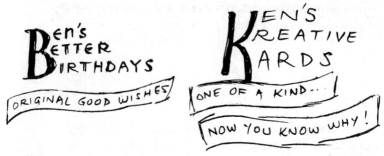

When organising blank cards (printers can cut up scrap card for you at a reasonable cost but you'll probably find what you want more easily at a stationery shop) make sure to get your envelopes first and then you know what size to get the cards.

Here's a nice folding 'pop-up' card which is simple to make.

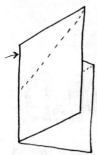

Fold the card like this. Then open and crease the vertical fold half way down in the reverse direction.

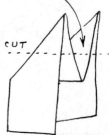

Then you can fold the card like this along the indicated dotted line. Then, if you cut right across where the dotted line is you get a card that opens up to reveal the inside, shaped like this.

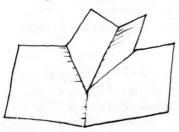

The outside of the card now looks like this.

Now cut across this dotted line.

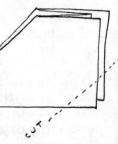

This now gives you a shape which by skilful drawing and painting can be made to look like a package.

On the inside you can draw a jack in the box so that when the card is opened out, up it pops! Surprise!!

You could cut around a shape to make it better.

The important thing is that you have made it and that it is specially for that person and that you've had fun and used your imagination and given someone some pleasure.

Enjoy it!

22

Develop your own style

I mentioned earlier that there are many different ways to draw.

A lot of people say, 'I couldn't draw a straight line.' I can safely say that drawing a straight line isn't that important, and if you *do* want to draw one, just put your paper along the edge of a table and, holding your pencil or pen exactly where you want the straight line to start, just run your hand down the page with your other fingers acting as a straight-line guide against the edge of the table.

What I started to say was that all you have to do is look at any publication which prints drawings or cartoons and you will see that there are a million different styles. As you go through life drawing your own cartoons, you should try to develop your own style.

You can borrow good ideas from other cartoonists, but try to be yourself. You may decide that ears do nothing to show expression so you will dispense with ears in all your drawings. Why not?

132

You may see some good sneaky-looking eyes and decide to use them. Do it!

You may realise that one artist always puts a pair of solid black trousers on the important figure in all his cartoons, while all the rest of that drawing is in a rather sketchy thin line: a good tip to take notice of.

You will see that some artists are superb in the way they draw anatomy, while others are very wooden. Some make a feature of doing what at first sight look like very babyish drawings; others are brilliant at drawing the surrounding buildings and background; while others specialise in horses, or dogs, or children. Each artist has successfully developed his or her style and you can learn from all of them.

The important thing is to create your own cartoons and have fun.

Here are as many bits and pieces of drawings and cartoons as I can find from different publications.

"Like I said, the four stars was for the petrol, not the food."

BARRY FANTONI

'How can you have wild life
without a disco?'

The GAMBOLS
by Barry Appleby

IT'S QUITE EASY

JUST WATCH ME AND DO EVERYTHING I DO

FRED BASSET
by GRAHAM

It's not my fault!

6763

© Associated Newspapers Group p.l.c. 1981

by Reg Smythe

"...turn left at the red socks, then straight on until you come to the striped pants and turn right, then..."

TEACH HIM TO STAND QUIETLY WHATEVER
YOU MAY BE DOING IN THE SADDLE

I STILL SAY WE SHOULDN'T HAVE
SOLD THE
TAPESTRY
RIGHTS

Just look at all the different styles. When you think of it
. . . there are a few there that you might have said 'gosh . . .
I could draw better than that!'

Do it, and I just hope you get as much fun as I do out of
drawing cartoons.

Cheers . . .

Acknowledgements

I would like to thank Marilyn Kneller, who helped me get the book past its first disorganised jottings. Her reactions, comments and enthusiasm were in a large part responsible for me starting the book.

Barry Appleby
Nick Baker
Hector Breeze (with thanks to *The Guardian*)
Barry Fantoni (with thanks to *The Times*)
Alex Graham (with thanks to Associated Newspapers)
Haro (with thanks to the *Daily Mail*)
Bindi Harris
Martin Honeysett (with thanks to *Punch*)
Dicky Howett (with thanks to the *Daily Mirror*)
Rachel Irving
Tom Johnston
David Langdon
Brian Reading (with thanks to the *Daily Mail*)
Reg Smythe (with thanks to the *Daily Mirror*)
Norman Thelwell

Why don't you
draw on these pages